A NEW AND APPROPRIATE SYSTEM OF EDUCATION
FOR THE LABOURING PEOPLE

The Development of Industrial Society Series

Patrick Colquhoun

A New and Appropriate System of
EDUCATION FOR THE
LABOURING PEOPLE

IRISH UNIVERSITY PRESS
Shannon   Ireland

First edition London 1806

ISBN 0 7165 1773 6

T M MacGlinchey Publisher

Irish University Press Shannon Ireland

PRINTED IN THE REPUBLIC OF IRELAND BY
ROBERT HOGG PRINTER TO IRISH UNIVERSITY PRESS

The Development of Industrial Society Series

This series comprises reprints of contemporary documents and commentaries on the social, political and economic upheavals in nineteenth-century England.

England, as the first industrial nation, was also the first country to experience the tremendous social and cultural impact consequent on the alienation of people in industrialized countries from their rural ancestry. The Industrial Revolution which had begun to intensify in the mid-eighteenth century, spread swiftly from England to Europe and America. Its effects have been far-reaching: the growth of cities with their urgent social and physical problems; greater social mobility; mass education; increasingly complex administration requirements in both local and central government; the growth of democracy and the development of new theories in economics; agricultural reform and the transformation of a way of life.

While it would be pretentious to claim for a series such as this an in-depth coverage of all these aspects of the new society, the works selected range in content from *The Hungry Forties* (1904), a collection of letters by ordinary working people describing their living conditions and the effects of mechanization on their day-to-day lives, to such analytical studies as Leone Levi's *History of British Commerce* (1880) and *Wages and Earnings of the Working Classes* (1885); M. T. Sadler's *The Law of Population* (1830); John Wade's radical documentation of government corruption, *The Extraordinary Black Book* (1831); C. Edward Lester's trenchant social investigation, *The Glory and Shame of England* (1866); and many other influential books and pamphlets.

The editor's intention has been to make available important contemporary accounts, studies and records, written or compiled by men and women of integrity and scholarship whose reactions to the growth of a new kind of society are valid touchstones for today's reader. Each title (and the particular edition used) has been chosen on a twofold basis (1) its intrinsic worth as a record or commentary, and (2) its contribution to the development of an industrial society. It is hoped that this collection will help to increase our understanding of a people and an epoch.

The Editor
Irish University Press

A NEW AND APPROPRIATE

SYSTEM OF EDUCATION

FOR THE LABOURING PEOPLE:

ELUCIDATED AND EXPLAINED, ACCORDING TO THE PLAN WHICH HAS
BEEN ESTABLISHED FOR THE

RELIGIOUS AND MORAL INSTRUCTION

OF MALE AND FEMALE CHILDREN,

ADMITTED INTO THE FREE SCHOOL, NO. 19, ORCHARD STREET,

IN THE CITY OF WESTMINSTER;

CONTAINING AN EXPOSITION OF

THE NATURE AND IMPORTANCE OF THE DESIGN,

AS IT RESPECTS THE GENERAL INTEREST OF THE COMMUNITY:

WITH DETAILS,

EXPLANATORY OF THE PARTICULAR ECONOMY OF THE INSTITUTION, AND
THE METHODS PRESCRIBED FOR THE PURPOSE OF SECURING AND
PRESERVING

A GREATER DEGREE OF MORAL RECTITUDE,

AS A MEANS OF PREVENTING CRIMINAL OFFENCES BY HABITS OF
TEMPERANCE, INDUSTRY, SUBORDINATION, AND LOYALTY,

AMONG THAT USEFUL CLASS OF THE COMMUNITY,

COMPRISING THE

LABOURING PEOPLE OF ENGLAND.

TO WHICH ARE ADDED,

CONCLUDING OBSERVATIONS,

ON THE

IMPORTANCE OF EXTENDING THE SYSTEM GENERALLY,

UNDER THE

AID AND SANCTION OF THE LEGISLATURE.

By P. COLQUHOUN,
LL.D.

LONDON:

PRINTED BY SAVAGE AND EASINGWOOD, BEDFORD BURY,
FOR J. HATCHARD, PICCADILLY;
AND SOLD BY THE BOOKSELLERS IN TOWN AND COUNTRY.

1806.

Price 2s. 6d.

ADVERTISEMENT.

————

THIS summary view of a practicable and economical System of Education, to be employed chiefly as a means of conveying to the children of the inferior classes of society an early and just sense of religion and moral rectitude, is given to the public, for the purpose of demonstrating the great importance of well-conducted designs of this nature, as they relate to the national prosperity, and the unquestionable interest of the community at large.

The subject will be found interesting in the point of view in which it has been placed, inasmuch as it explains all that is necessary for giving effect to this new System of Education wherever it may be adopted.

If the impressions, which may be conveyed through this medium, shall produce a disposition on the part of the Legislature to accomplish the great object of a National Education for the Children of the Poor; or if they shall generally stimulate opulent and respectable individuals, wherever they may have local influence, to promote the same benevolent design—the Author will consider himself as amply repaid in the incalculable benefits which will thereby result to his country.

London, 21st August, 1806.

CONTENTS.

APPENDIX.

INTRODUCTION,

Containing Details respecting the Free School in Westminster, and the Advantages which would result from a General Adoption of the System throughout the Kingdom.

THE promoters of this institution have seen, with the deepest regret, that in what is called the City of Westminster, comprising only two parishes, there are not less at any time than two thousand children, in the course of advancing to an adult state, who are rearing up in the grossest ignorance*—who have no means of

---

* It appears by the Parliamentary returns of the population obtained in 1803, that in the City of Westminster, so called, comprizing the parishes of St. Margaret and St. John the Evangelist, there are 7502 families, composed of 10,744 males, and 15,139 females, total 25,883. There appears to be nearly three females to two males, but this arises in part from the soldiers being enumerated separately. It has been calculated, that this population includes about 6000 children, at an age to receive education; of these 4000 are supposed to be sent to different schools, and that the remaining 2000 without assistance must be reared up in the grossest ignorance either of religious or moral instruction. This observation applies to every poor neighbourhood in the metropolis—and the number of children so circumstanced may be about 50,000.

receiving religious or moral instruction in their early years—who have in general the worst possible examples daily before them, and who, as they advance to maturity, become victims to those vices, which not only entail misery and ruin upon themselves, but render them bad and noxious members of society, instead of becoming good servants, and labourers, or useful handicrafts; and there is no doubt of the youth of both sexes, in every district of the metropolis where the inferior orders of society are congregated, being nearly in the same deplorable situation.

The City of Westminster, however, in some respects, differs from the other districts, inasmuch as the children of soldiers are very numerous, and the Asylum at Chelsea, notwithstanding its extended scale, has been found insufficient to compass more than a part of the whole; and but for this institution a considerable number must be reared to maturity in vice and ignorance*.

* It appears from a calculation made early in 1802, that in the three Regiments of Guards, there were 2250 wives, and about 3300 children, one third of which, or about 1100 are supposed at all times fit for school. In the whole army it is calculated, that there are about 54,000 children

Numberless instances occur in this nation, and particularly in the metropolis, where benevolent individuals are employed in administering relief to distress under every shape which it assumes. But the higher and noble aim of preventing those calamities which lead to idleness and crimes, and produce poverty and misery, by guiding and properly directing the early conduct of the lower orders of the community, and by giving a right bias to their minds, has not, as yet, generally attracted the notice of those who move in the more elevated walks of life; nor has its importance been sufficiently estimated, as it regards society at large, considering the changes in manners and habits which are rapidly taking place, although, perhaps, not obvious to the mass of the community, whose attention is seldom directed to the retrograde progress of the moral habits of the poor; but the fact is no less true, that there never existed a period in our history, where an attention to the rising generation among the

in time of war, and of these upwards of 16,000 require education. The Military Asylum at Chelsea, can therefore only compass a very small part of the whole, and even the children of the soldiers of the Guards cannot all get admission.—At present there are 131 soldiers' children in Westminster School, taught free of expense.

lower classes of society, became an object of greater importance to the nation at large. The prosperity of every state depends on the good habits, and the religious and moral instruction of the labouring people. By shielding the minds of youth against the vices that are most likely to beset them, much is gained to society in the prevention of crimes, and in lessening the demand for punishments. The laws have done much to punish offences: It remains yet to do much for prevention. This desideratum, of such incalculable importance to the great interests of society, is best attained by giving proper instruction to the inferior classes in early life.

It is not, however, proposed by this institution, that the children of the poor should be educated in a manner to elevate their minds above the rank they are destined to fill in society, or that an expense should be incurred beyond the lowest rate ever paid for instruction. Utopian schemes for an extensive diffusion of knowledge would be injurious and absurd. A right bias to their minds, and a sufficient education to enable them to preserve, and to estimate properly, the religious and moral instruction they receive, is all that

is, or ought ever to be, in contemplation.
To go beyond this point would be to con-
found the ranks of society upon which the
general happiness of the lower orders, no less
than those that are more elevated, depends;
since by indiscriminate education those destined for laborious occupations would become discontented and unhappy in an inferior situation of life, which, however, when for-
tified by virtue, and stimulated by industry, is
not less happy than what is experienced by
those who move in a higher sphere, of whose
cares they are ignorant, and with many of
whose anxieties and distresses they are never
assailed.

In this point of view the education con
templated, and which has for some years
been put in practice with respect to the
children admitted into the Free School, in
Orchard Street, Westminster, is of the highest importance; and its general diffusion
throughout the whole kingdom would perhaps
be the greatest boon which could be conferred on the community at large.

But in order to compass this object, even
on a limited scale, and at an expense which
is practicable, and within the reach of local

benevolence, the old mode of educating the youth of the poor must be totally abandoned, and the whole design conducted upon one system.

The nation is indebted to the genius, the ability, and persevering industry, of the Rev. Dr. Bell, late Superintendant and Director of the Male Asylum, at Madras, in the East Indies, and now Rector of Swanage, in Dorsetshire, for a most enlightened plan of education for the poor, which he some time since disclosed to the public; and for which he deserves a statue to his memory. It is upon this plan chiefly that the Free School, in Orchard Street, will be conducted. The school house has lately undergone several improvements, so as to afford accommodation to about 230 boys, and 170 girls; making in the whole 400 pupils, to be taught under the superintendance of one master for the boys, and one mistress for the girls, in schools under the same roof; but totally unconnected with each other.

EXPLANATION OF THE SYSTEM, AS IT RELATES TO THE TEACHERS.

According to the system which has been adopted, the pupils who have discovered talents are selected by the master and mistress, as tutors to those in the same class, who are yet to be taught what these tutors already know, and so on from the lowest to the highest class in the school; the best informed and the most capable of the boys and girls are to be employed in teaching the others ; and in the progress of this employment, by which they are raised in their own estimation to consequence in the school, they are at the same time instructing themselves in a manner rapid beyond conception. Emulation is excited between one tutor and another; the minds of the whole are constantly employed in the task assigned to each; and their zeal is increased by the confidence reposed in them by the master and mistress.

In addition to the tutors, each class should as soon as possible be furnished with a *monitor* or usher, selected from the most capable of the boys or girls who are farthest advanced in their education, and to whom should be assigned the task of guiding and directing the tutors, and to see that strict attention is given to the lessons which are prescribed, and that the most rigid discipline and good order are maintained. These superior teachers are also improving themselves while they are exercising their different classes in the various branches of education in which they are progressively engaged.

The province of the master and mistress is to direct the whole machine in all its parts— to prescribe the mode of instruction according to the progress that is made; to arrange the classes in the manner best calculated to facilitate the great object in view, by a judicious selection of those whose advancement is nearly equal, and to see that the various offices assigned to the tutors and monitors are duly and accurately executed. It is their business to see that others work, rather than work themselves. The master and mistress, from their respective chairs, overlook every part of the school, and give life and motion to the whole. They inspect the classes one after another; call upon the monitors occasionally to bring them up, that they may specifically examine the progress of each pupil, and where deficiencies are discovered, or ad-

vancement in education manifested, they re-
duce the deficient to an under, and those more
advanced to the upper class, so that in point
of progress the whole may at all times not
only be upon a par, but that emulation may
thereby also be excited. It is the duty of the
master and mistress to encourage the *diffident*,
the *timid*, and the *backward;* to check and
repress the *forward* and *presumptuous*—to bestow just and ample commendation upon the
diligent, *attentive*, and *orderly*, however dull
their capacity, or slow their progress; to stimulate the *ambitious*, rouse the *indolent*, and
to correct the *slothfulness of the idle:*—To
deal out *praise, encouragement*, and *threatening*,
according to the *temper, disposition*, and *genius* of the *pupil*.

One of the chief objects of the system is to
prevent waste of time in the schools:—to
render the condition of the pupils pleasant to
themselves; and to lead their attention to the
objects in which they are engaged, namely,
to instruct and ground them in that portion
of education which is necessary to convey
religious and moral principles. To impress
their minds strongly with a horror of those
vices to which their situations in life more

particularly expose them:—a love of *truth*,
honesty, and every moral virtue; and above
all, a strong sense of *religion*, carefully instill-
ed according to the rules prescribed by the
national church. In fine, so to fortify their
minds as, if possible, to render them proof
against those vices and temptations to which
their situations, particularly in large cities, expose them, and thereby to render them good
and useful members of the community in the
inferior situations of life which they are destined to fill.

In the general progress of education, it is
also the duty of the master and mistress to
stimulate the pupils by rewards rather than punishments; for which purpose appropriate toys
for the youngest, and prize books, and other useful articles for those that are farther advanced,
with medals and other badges of honour for
those who particularly distinguish themselves,
should be provided by the managers, and
distributed by the president or chairman of
the committee, who may periodically view
and examine the boys' school, or by the ladies who shall benevolently undertake to visit
and superintend the school for the girls; and
it will be the duty of the master and mistress to

provide a *prize ticket*, to be numbered No. 1. and upwards, to be delivered to each boy and girl for every meritorious act they perform, whether it relates to *general good behaviour, attention, assiduity, progress in education*, or *punctual attendance at school*. Such particular acts of merit to be written or printed on each ticket, and delivered to the pupils, that they may receive a reward according to the number of tickets they produce, denoting the degree of merit they are thus found to possess; and such rewards to be distributed quarterly, or oftener, if it shall be so determined by the committee of managers.

It will be of the greatest importance that the master and mistress bestow particular attention to the training of the *tutors* and *monitors;* but particularly the latter, as every thing depends on their fitness for the important task assigned them; not only as it regards the discipline and general economy of the school, and the success of the design, but as it respects the ease and comfort of the master and mistress themselves, since without system and method, well arranged, and vigorously and attentively enforced, the general superintendance will become a source of *pain and anxiety*, instead of great pleasure and comfort; and it ought to be recollected by every master and mistress, that the system or scheme of education now proposed, is neither *visionary* nor *Utopian*.—It has been tried, and proved to be effectual and practicable; and therefore in all cases where it does not completely succeed, the blame will attach to those who conduct the design, and not to the system itself.

With a view therefore to derive those public benefits, which are expected from the exertions of the monitors, upon which so much depends, it is proposed, that in addition to the prizes which they will receive in common with all the pupils and tutors employed in the school, they shall be entitled to certain small pecuniary gratuities or rewards, besides honorary badges of distinction, for assiduity and success in their different duties—as *good teachers, attentive monitors, progressive advancement in their own education, and punctual and regular attendance at the school;* and for each of these acts of merit they will receive separate tickets from the master, from time to time, expressing his sense of their services, which shall be denominated *money tickets.*—According to which the chairman of the visiting committee shall reward them quarterly.—And besides, will ornament them with medals, or badges of honour, according to their respective merits.

For the purpose also of correcting *idleness, inattention, and bad behaviour,* or *absence from school,* without a just cause assigned by the parents of the children, it is proposed, that two books shall be kept; one by the master, and another by the mistress, which in each school shall be called the *black book,* in which shall be distinctly registered alphabetically, the *misconduct* and *bad behaviour* of each boy and girl in the two schools, specifying the nature of the offence—whether uttering a *profane oath, lying, cheating, truant, idleness, negligence,* attending school without being combed and washed, or any other fault requiring investigation and animadversion, which book must not only be submitted to the periodical visitors, but also laid before the managers at the quarterly examination of the schools, and the culprits particularly summoned with their parents to attend, that they may have an admonition from the president or chairman, and that those who are incorrigible, and likely to corrupt the other pupils, may be expelled the school—but not (in the boys' school) until a jury of 24 of the scholars, taken from the three highest classes, (8 out of each) shall by their verdict determine that such culprit or culprits is or are unworthy of the great benefits derived from the school, and that their bad example and highly improper conduct must prove injurious if they are not expelled.

This check upon delinquency is proposed with an immediate view to promote good order, diligence, and rigid discipline, at the least expense of punishment, of which it is a great object to be frugal and a good economist.

Every act of delinquency deserving a place in the *black book* is to be immediately marked on the slate by the tutor or monitor, for the consideration of the master or mistress, whether it deserves a place there or not, and if the tutor shall neglect to mark such act of delinquency, and shall fail to give notice of it to the monitor, he or she, so neglecting, shall be marked in the *black book*, and so shall the monitor if he or she neglects to inform the master or mistress of the delinquency disclosed by the tutors, or by any pupil in the school.

Experience has already shown that a strict adherence to this rule has had a most excellent effect in producing attention and good order.—But for the purpose of rendering it effectually useful, it will be the duty of the master and mistress, once in every week, in presence of the whole school, solemnly to inspect and scrutinize the faults of all culprits who are thus registered, when the nature and consequence of every *omission* and *commission* shall be explained in plain and familiar language, suited to the comprehension of all the pupils, with proper commentaries, and an appropriate admonition as it applies to each offence.

Checks of this nature (where those assigned to conduct the affairs of the school, as well as the pupils themselves, are bound to report whatever they see done amiss, contrary to the rules established for its good government, and where they themselves are liable to be disgraced if they neglect their duty) by securing the detection of delinquency, tend in an eminent degree to prevent carelessness and irregularity, and to establish good habits both in, and out of school.

SYSTEM OF EDUCATION IN THE BOYS' SCHOOL.

For the purpose of facilitating education, the reading and writing department of the school is divided into eight or more classes, and each pupil is furnished in the first instance with a slate and pencil; but to save expense, *refuse slates* are procured, generally gratis, where new buildings are erecting, and the boys are afterwards employed in grinding the surface smooth, so as to admit of letters and figures being marked or written upon them: each pupil therefore begins to mark, or write, at the moment he begins to learn his alphabet. This idea is taken from a practice observed by Dr. Bell, in a Malabar School, in the East Indies, with this difference, that instead of marking the letters on sand, they are formed by a pencil on the slate. Great advantages arise from teaching the alphabet in this manner; it engages and amuses the mind, and so commands the attention of the young pupil, that it greatly facilitates the toil both of the tutor and the scholar, to whom it gives a distinct and accurate idea of the shape and form of each letter, while it enables the pupil, at the very outset, to distinguish the letters of a similar cast or form, such as b, d, p, and q. In fact, it removes every obstacle which at first puzzles the young beginner and interrupts his progress. And experience has evinced, that, by the adoption of this mode of teaching, the progress is rapid beyond all example; since by following it up with accuracy, pupils have been taught both to read and write, distinctly, in the course of twelve months. In fact, reading and writing, (the latter generally upon the slate,) are rendered subservient to each other, in the whole progress of this humble, though useful system of moderate and cheap education. It is *cheap*, because one master or mistress, of proper abilities, while the pupils are thus made to instruct one another, may each superintend and perfect the instruction of 500 children, which, according to the old mode, required the labour of at least a dozen of different teachers, and as many salaries. It is cheap, also, because slates (unless during a short period before quitting school) are substituted for paper and books, in teaching writing and arithmetic. The saving in quills, and particularly in school books, is immense, inasmuch as not one hundredth part is necessary according to this new and improved method of educating the children of the poor; and upon the whole it may be fairly estimated, that on a scale of 500 pupils the greatest aggregate expense for each, including *school-master's salary, books, prizes, medals, pecuniary rewards, rent of school house, &c.* can scarce exceed ten shillings a year for each pupil. A sum so very small as to be within the reach of private benevolence in all instances where persons of opulence reside in the district, and where the circumstances of the parents cannot compass this very inconsiderable expense*, which with day labourers is very frequently the case.

---

* In the Seminary in Orchard Street, Westminster, the children of soldiers, and all orphan pupils, are taught gratis. The children of persons not coming under the above description, pay as follows :—

If one child, 1s. per calendar month on advance.
If two children of the same family 1s. 10d.   Idem.
If three children, 2s. 6d.   Idem.
If four children, 3s.   Idem.

Having said thus much in elucidation of the first principles of the design, it becomes necessary to give as short and comprehensive a view of the detail, as it applies to the progress of the education of the pupils, as the limits of this work will admit.

The plan of the boys' school admits of a division into eight different classes, although circumstances may render it necessary sometimes to abridge, and at other times to extend that number.

The First Class is confined solely to the alphabet, A, B, C, &c. each pupil having a tutor farther advanced to instruct him, and facilitate his progress in learning the letters. A knowledge of which, by the assistance of the slate, and by marking the letters, is very soon acquired, with the aid of a superintending monitor, who ought to have the letters of the alphabet, on pasteboard, suspended from his neck.

The Second Class is limited to pupils exercised in words of two letters, with the same assistance, each marking the letters on the slate, and then giving the sound.

The Third Class. Idem of three letters.

The Fourth Class. Idem of four letters.

The Fifth Class. Idem of five or more letters.

The Sixth Class reads, in rotation, the Psalter, New Testament, and other appropriate books of instruction, aided by tutors and a superintending monitor.

The Seventh Class reads the Old Testament, and other books of instruction suitable to their progress, with the same assistance.

The Eighth Class, which comprises the best readers, are exercised under a fit monitor, in reading, in rotation, portions of Scripture,

also well-selected books, suited
to their progress and to their
future pursuits in life, with a
view to fix in their minds,
strong incitements to religion
and virtue; to *truth, honesty,
peaceable demeanour in society,
industry, sobriety, subordination and loyalty**.

SPELLING.

The first rudiments of spelling, in order
to save books, are acquired by printing the
words, which are introduced into the common spelling books, beginning from words of
the lowest to the highest syllables, in a large
type, on one side of a sheet of paper, and
then pasting each on pasteboard, by which
one of such cards will suffice for twenty boys
properly placed or disposed in the school, so

---

* In reading, the pupils read lines, or sentences, and
sometimes paragraphs, in rotation, in a slow and delibe-
rate manner, the previous instruction in progressive spelling,
prepares them for thus reading one after another in the
same book, by which much expense is saved, and the
destruction of a number of books prevented, by *thumbing*
and otherwise.

that the whole may inspect it. And by changing from class to class, will answer the purpose of 500 books, and will last much longer. It has been calculated that, at least, 150 pupils may repeat their respective lessons from one of these cards, in the space of about an hour, or less.

When the pupils are a little advanced, an extempore mode of spelling may be resorted to with considerable advantage. With a view to this exercise, the monitor points out the columns of spelling, which form the lesson for the day. One of the pupils is required by him to read, distinctly, six or more words by syllables, repeating each syllable in every word. If he commits a mistake, recourse is had to the next pupil in rotation, and so on until a pupil is found who will rectify it, and he of course takes place of those who preceded him. If the whole class shall happen to commit the same or a similar mistake, then such mistake is disclosed by the monitor to the pupils, but not otherwise. According to this rule, each pupil is made to teach himself, and it is the principal duty of the monitor in this, as in most cases, to see that they teach one another.

When the pupils have thus read over the words which compose the lesson of the day, the monitor's duty then is to take up the card, and require each of the class to spell such words as he repeats to them. And emulation is kept up by giving the correct spellers a place over those that are faulty. To facilitate this species of instruction, the pupils generally spell in rotation, and one great apvantage attending it is, that it forms an excellent auxiliary to the method of spelling on the slate, which is hereafter explained. But in this, as in every thing else, much depends on the attention of the monitor, and the superintendance of the master, as by the least omission in performing any part of this duty, the pupils are deranged, and their minds are diverted from the object immediately in view.

It becomes, therefore, the bounden duty of the master or mistress in this, as in all other cases, to see that the monitors are properly instructed, and perform the various duties assigned them correctly; and these duties being visible, the check should be immediately applied, since without good and well-trained monitors, according to this system, it can never be made so effectual, as the general scheme admits, in rendering the progress of the pupils useful to themselves, and to the community at large.

After the pupils are sufficiently advanced in spelling, with a tolerable degree of correctness, they may be formed into occasional classes: with a view to prove their proficiency, each having his slate and pencil in readiness, the monitor of the class pronounces aloud the word to be written by the whole class, and produced immediately to the monitor; or several words are written one after another, and then the whole is examined by the monitor, and occasionally by the master, who corrects the false spelling, and explains, familiarly, the principle to be adopted in true spelling. In this exercise one spelling-book, or card containing the words held in the monitor's hand, is all that is necessary, and the progress is found to be much more rapid, than if the expense of a spelling book for each were incurred, while the attention is more fixed, and all sluggishness prevented, by the emulation which is thus excited between one pupil and another.

In addition to these different modes, every class, at the end of each lesson in reading, may be required, in rotation, to spell (off book) every word with which they are not supposed to be familiar, but not by the mode of dividing the syllables, which becomes a waste of time when the pupils are further advanced, and a protraction of habits, which are only applicable to young beginners, and ultimately not well calculated to obtain a perfect knowledge of orthography.

WRITING.

It has already been observed, that according to this new mode of education, writing and reading go hand in hand, and assist each other in the progress of the pupils, who first begin to mark the letters of the alphabet on slates, and next to join them, and afterwards to make numerical figures, preparatory to their learning a little of arithmetic. The practice thus acquired by writing every day upon the slate, produces a proficiency, in a short time, which is truly astonishing: and this species of education is obtained without the expense of paper, pens, or ink, by which the saving is in the proportion of about

£800 a year, for 500 pupils, while in addition to this advantage, in point of economy, it is calculated that each scholar, within the year, has about five or six times the practice which the old expensive mode affords. But in the progress of thus learning to write well, attention is paid by the monitors, under the direction of the master, to the mode of holding the slate pencil, and, afterwards, before the pupils ultimately leave the school, to the best method of holding and making pens, ruling paper, and of writing thereon with ease and advantage, inasmuch, as it differs, in some respects, from his previous instruction in writing on the slate.

The great desideratum in this mode of education is to make the pupil do every thing for himself. No person, on any pretence, should be permitted to make a pen, rule a line, or do any thing whatever on the slate, or copy book, of any scholar. It is by such means only, that pupils can be expected to make progress in their education.

In the Free School, in Orchard Street, the specimens of writing, which have been exhibited by the pupils upon their slates, indicate a progress which is truly surprising; and some of them have actually acquired a knowledge of reading and writing, sufficient for the walks of life they are destined to fill, in the course of a single year.

ARITHMETIC.

This branch of education is taught, also, upon a new principle; calculated, in an eminent degree, to facilitate the progress of the scholar; but, unless in cases where great talents are discovered, or with a view to educate monitors, for the purpose of becoming, afterwards, school-masters and teachers according to this new system, the object of the managers of this institution does not extend further than to teach the pupils the first four rules of arithmetic. The method adopted by Mr. Lancaster, at his Free School, in the Borough Road, Southwark, and explained in his book, entitled *Improvements in Education*, published 1805, from page 62 to 85, in that work, appears well adapted to the object in view.

The pupils are arranged into 12 classes, from the lowest to the highest.

The 1st Class is taught the combination of figures, which they write on their slates, as dictated by their monitor.

  2 Class Addition—which is written also on the slate, as dictated by the monitor

3 Class	Compound Addition	Idem
4 Class	Subtraction	Idem
5 Class	Compound Subtraction	Idem
6 Class	Multiplication	Idem
7 Class	Compound Multiplication	Idem
8 Class	Division	Idem
9 Class	Compound Division	Idem
10 Class	Reduction	Idem
11 Class	Rule of Three	Idem
12 Class	Practice	Idem

According to this plan the classes of the school undergo a new and distinct arrangement applicable to this particular branch of education, and are distributed according to the progress they have made in arithmetic. At the precise time appointed for this branch, the school separate from their reading classes, and combine together in their proper order, and remain in distinct classes until their tasks are finished—and then they again reunite according to the arrangements established for the reading classes; by a due attention to the discipline of the school, upon which every thing depends, these changes are, or ought to be, effected without noise or trouble in the course of a few minutes. Such pupils as have not begun to cipher remain during this arrangement under the care of the monitors for instruction in reading; but in general, all pupils who can read and write text-hand in four letters, are introduced into the first class; and experience has shown, that according to this method boys have been taught arithmetic and writing in six or nine months, who never handled a slate pencil, or a pen, before.

Every rule in arithmetic is considered as a study appointed for every separate class according to their progress, and they never advance until they are perfect in the branch to which the attention of the pupils is directed. According to this method, whatever the number of pupils may be, the trouble of tuition is not increased—every pupil in each class is told by the monitor what task he is to perform—it is before him on his slate, and it is his sole business to do it, over and over again, until he is perfect.

Having advanced a certain length, it becomes the business of the pupils to do every thing without the instruction of the monitor. To each class is allotted a proper sum or exercise according to the arithmetical rule which they are practising at the time. The sums applicable to each class (which for convenience ought not to exceed 12) is written upon a board with chalk, or upon a card with ink, which' is either suspended from the wall, or placed in such a position as to be seen by each respective class. The monitors who superintend, have previously ascertained what the result of each problem or example ought to be, whether in *Addition, Subtraction, Multiplication, Division, Reduction, the Rule of Three, or Practice.* After the task is complete in each class, the result is called out by each pupil, and those that are correct take precedence of the others. In cases where many mistakes occur, such pupils are required to return to their primary mode of instruction until they are rendered more perfect. In both instances the great advantage is, that neither the teacher, or pupil can be a moment idle. In this case, as in all others, in the progress of this new system of education, the spirit of emulation is kept up two ways—first, by obtaining precedence in the class; second, by prize tickets, which, as has already been observed, entitle the meritorious pupil to an honorary reward from the periodical visitors of the school for quick progress in different branches of education. And thus may arithmetic be taught, as far as is necessary for the inferior classes of society, without the expense of books or paper. In this branch, as well as in others, it may be useful to the master and mistress to make themselves acquainted with the minute details and explanations given in the work before mentioned, not only with respect to arithmetic alone, but also to spelling and reading*.

RELIGIOUS AND MORAL INSTRUCTION.

The great and primary object of this institution is, that the pupils, both male and

* In this general exposition of the system of education, a wider range is marked out than may be absolutely necessary to adopt for the Children of the Poor, and certainly beyond the views of the Author, whose object extends no farther than to give that portion of instruction which shall strongly impress religious and moral duties on the minds of the vulgar. These details, however, may prove useful in economising education in general with respect to classes of a rank somewhat superior.

female, should be strongly impressed with a just sense of religion and morality. With this view it is an indispensable rule in the Westminster seminary, that devotional exercises *in strict unison with the established church*, and in a manner suited to the capacity of the youth of both sexes, and to the vices which are likely to assail them, shall be performed in the school, when assembled and dismissed every day; and that those who have been taught, shall join in a short and appropriate hymn, or one or more verses of a psalm, suited to the purpose.

It is also required of the master or mistress, when any irreligious, criminal, immoral, or improper act, such as *picking and stealing*, *unlawfully pawning*, *swearing*, *lying*, *dissimulation*, *cheating*, *obscene expressions*, *rudeness*, *a disposition to quarrel*, *cruelty to animals*, *absence from school without a just cause*, *disobedience to parents or relations*, *or others under whose care they are placed*, and all other offences of *a bad tendency* are discovered, that each offence shall be registered in the *black book*, and dealt with immediately according to the extent of its turpitude or malignity, by a solemn appeal from the master or mistress to the whole school, representing, in language suitable to the comprehension of the children, the shocking consequences which must result to the culprits from a repetition of the same offence, in all the different shapes which the nature of the case may require, and warning all the others to beware the like, and all other offences, contrary to the *will of God,* and to the *laws of the school,* which are hereafter detailed, bringing to their recollection, at the same time, what they are taught in the *church catechism,* the *scriptures,* and other good books, and how necessary it is for their own happiness and comfort, when they grow up, that they should be *good men* and *good women,* and that the pains now bestowed to give them proper instruction is for their benefit alone, not only in this world, but in that which is to come. In short, every instance of ill behaviour which occurs, is to be seized upon by the master and mistress, for the purpose of offering good and wholesome admonition to the children. As the impression it will make upon their minds, when rendered applicable to particular acts of irreligious, criminal, or immoral conduct, will be strongly felt, and will operate more powerfully on their present and future conduct in life, than any thing that can be taught in the way of lessons.

SUNDAY EXERCISES.

It is indispensably necessary that both the pupils and monitors should attend the school every Sunday, both in the morning and evening, not only to join in devotional exercises, according to the forms prescribed by the established church, but also according to a form adapted more particularly to the understandings of the younger pupils ; where responses, so necessary to fix the attention, are likewise introduced. A portion of this day is also to be employed according to the most approved and facile method, in perfecting each pupil in the church catechism, and in a moderate knowledge of psalmody. And no excuse must be admitted on the part of any pupil, male or female, unless it can be clearly ascertained, that they accompany their parents to some place of public worship, and that they have completely learned their catechism.

When the school is thus convened, it will be the duty of the master and mistress, either extempore, or by reading from proper books, to descant on the benefits which will result to the children from following up the excellent precepts contained in the church cate- chism.

It is proposed, after the system is sufficient- ly perfect, and the major part of the children are further advanced in religious knowledge, that they shall accompany the master and mis- tress twice a day on Sunday to the established church, and afterwards spend an hour in the school, for the purpose of instruction in re- ligion, and of hearing the observations of the master and mistress on the nature and mean- ing of the service prescribed for the day, and on the sermons which were preached.

THE LAWS OF THE SCHOOL.

After prayers, every Saturday morning, it will be the duty of the master or mistress, either to read themselves, or cause to be read, with an audible voice, the following laws and regulations of the school.

1. All scholars shall appear at the school punctually at nine in the morning,

clean washed and combed, with their
hair cut short, and head clean. They
shall remain in school until twelve.—
They are again to return punctually at
two o'clock, and remain until five, excepting on Wednesdays and Saturdays,
which are half-holidays, and on these
days they are to remain in school until
one, and not to return in the afternoon.

2. All scholars shall in like manner attend
on Sunday, from ten till twelve in the
morning, and from two till four in the
afternoon, with clean shirts, washed and
combed, and in their best clothes, unless their parents or friends will posi-
tively engage to take them to some
place of public worship, twice on that
day.

3. All scholars, during the whole of the
school hours, shall attend diligently to
the lessons, and shall be attentive to the
master, the monitors, and the tutors who
are set over them, always recollecting
that they have been sent to school to
learn what is good and useful to themselves, and with a view to their happi-

ness and prosperity in this life and that which is to come, after they die.

4. Every scholar shall preserve the utmost silence and quietness during school hours.

5. Every scholar who is absent from school, without the leave of the master, will lose the benefit thereof, and be excluded and turned out with disgrace, and never admitted again; unless the absence has been occasioned by sickness, or some other reasonable cause, to be stated by the parents.

6. All scholars receiving the benefits of this school must not only behave well when they are in it, but they must also be orderly and discreet when they are out of doors. They are not to offend the Great God their Maker, by *cursing* and *swearing*, because they may hear grown persons commit this great sin. They are not to cheat, to *tell lies*, to *quarrel or abuse* one another, or call one another *bad names*. They are not to *use acts of cruelty, even to the smallest*

animal.—They are not to learn, or sing, *bad songs*, and, above all, they are not to *associate and play, or to keep company, with wicked or bad children, whether boys or girls, who make use of bad words,* who are guilty of *picking and stealing, swearing, telling lies, cheating, playing at bad games for money, drinking in ale houses,* and keeping company with bad women: as all these acts of great wickedness are known to be *evil communications which corrupt good manners,* and are a sure road to the gallows, or to some severe and disgraceful punishment. Beware therefore of running about the streets, and forming an acquaintance with idle, disorderly, and bad children, out of school hours, particularly on the Lord's Day; stay at home on that holy day, read your books, and endeavour to give pleasure to your parents and friends, by showing the progress you have made in your learning—and in every thing that is good and praiseworthy, which you have been taught at the school.

7. As prizes will be given to every scholar, by the gentlemen and ladies who exa-

mine the school, according to the number of tickets which you may receive
from the master for *good behaviour in*
and *out of school—attention to your duties*
when in school, and *advancement in learn-*
ing: struggle therefore to outdo each
other, that you may have many prizes;
always considering that the good scholar, who runs fastest in pursuit of learning, always gets the best of all prizes,
because nothing is so good as learning
to young persons, such as they obtain
at this school; because it tends to make
them good, happy, and comfortable all
their lives.

8. It is expected that all the scholars admitted into this school, shall, before go-
ing to bed in the evening, first recollect
all the faults they have committed during the day; and afterwards, that they
will say their prayers according to the
form which has been delivered to them,
and also a morning prayer, immediately
after they get up out of bed, which will
be found printed in the same paper,
both which they must get by heart, as
soon as possible—and repeat the same

in the school every Sunday, that the master may know they have learnt their prayers.

9. The great duty of all children, and it is a duty particularly expected of those who are admitted into this school, is, that they shall attend to the Divine precept, *Fear God, and honour the King, and all in authority under him*—that they are dutiful and obedient to their parents and friends who have the charge of them, and thankful to them for sending them to school.—That they abstain from all vice and wickedness, and do honour to the school in which they are taught, by showing a good example to all other children who have not the same benefits.

10. All offences against these good laws will be marked down in the black book, and submitted to the inspection of the visitors, that they may be able to distinguish the good from the bad scholars, and wherever a fault is committed by any one, so as to be placed in the black book, all the tickets before received with

a view to a prize will be for ever for-
feited; and no prize will be given by the
visitors, where the *black book* records
any fault. Take care, therefore, that none
of your names get upon the *black book*.

ADDITIONAL SYSTEM OF EDUCATION, AP-PLICABLE TO THE GIRLS' SCHOOL.

The general rules laid down as they relate
to education, and to religious and moral instruction, apply in most instances to both
schools; but there are other regulations pe-
culiarly applicable to the girls' school which
it is necessary to explain. Since, in addition
to the different branches of education which
have been already mentioned, which however
admit of some variations more immediately applicable to females, it has been a desideratum
to employ a certain portion of their time in *nee-
dle work*, and other *suitable female employments*,
calculated to enable them to gain their living
as menial servants, or in some other reputable
and useful employment. With this view, it is
considered as the duty of the mistress, through
the medium of tutors and monitors, as far as
such a system can be rendered applicable
to females—to teach them *to sew*, to *make and
mend their own clothes, to mark, and to knit stock-*

ings. Straw plat may be also introduced, that they may possess as many resources as possible for gaining a livelihood in an honest way; but the great object is, to fit them for domestic situations, and to make them good servants*, by fortifying their minds against those vices to which they are more particularly exposed —to guard them against seduction, and to impress upon their minds the utmost horror of a state of female prostitution; to warn them against associating with bad women of this description, by frequent admonitions, depicting in strong colours the miseries, the distresses, and the crimes to which such bad examples will lead.—To show them, that a *love of idleness*, finery, and dress, an impatience under restraint in servitude, an indisposition to do their duty as good servants, an instability of temper, which will not permit them to listen to just and proper reproof, or admonition from masters or mistresses, when the duty they are bound to perform is neglected, sends many young women, who thoughtlessly

* With this view they will be employed in washing the school house and stairs, and other domestic employments, suited to their strength, as far as the system will permit; and small premiums will be given to excite emulation in these employments. They have been, and will be, employed also in making shifts, frocks and petticoats of different sizes, from materials furnished by the managers at the ready

gave up good places, into the streets, and entail upon them misery and wretchedness as long as they live.—To assure them that the moment they forget the good precepts learnt at school, and cease to be *prudent, industrious, careful,* and *discreet,* that their ruin and misery become certain.

Admonitions extending to these specific points are of the greatest importance in the metropolis and most large towns, where the vices of their own sex are in a manner rendered familiar from early years by too frequent intercourse with women of depraved manners in many instances unavoidable (it is to be feared) in vulgar life, where numbers of every description herd together in miserable lodgings, by which vice, and profligacy, is too often rendered familiar to young female minds, before they have been able to make the distinction between good and bad morals; and hence it is, that so many females become miserable and abandoned prostitutes, *even* before they arrive at an adult age.

money wholesale prices, and, when made up, the parents are, and will be, invited to purchase the garments made by their own children, at the first cost only of the materials, and an attempt is thus made of ultimately clothing all the girls in cheap decent dresses made by themselves, all of the same pattern.

*Copy of a Printed Address, on a paper apart, deli-
vered to each of the Parents of Children admitted
into the Free School, in Orchard Street, Westminster, as a farther means of promoting regu-
larity and good discipline, and presented to the
Author by a benevolent Subscriber.*

THE visitors who superintend the school are
anxious to train up the children educated
there in habits of diligence and good order,
cleanliness and neatness; in principles of morality and religion, and in obedience to their
parents; that they may be prepared to fulfil
the duties of the stations in which they may
be hereafter placed. In this good design
you are earnestly invited to act in concert
with them; for it will be in vain to give instruction at school, if it is not seconded by
the endeavours of Parents at home.

You are entreated, then, to be very careful
that your children attend the school punctually at the appointed hour, not suffering
them to trifle till it is late, or to loiter by the
way. Let them be always clean washed and
combed, that they may learn to be ashamed
of not being neat and cleanly. Do not permit them to be absent from school, except
upon occasions of absolute necessity, for those
who are frequently absent can never make
much progress. You are earnestly requested

also not to allow them to run about the streets out of school hours, or to form acquaintance with idle and disorderly children: and particularly on the Sunday, out of the hours of attendance at school and at church, keep them at home, under your own eye, and see that they are properly employed.

A little reflection will convince you of the absolute necessity of fully submitting to all the regulations of the school, and of supporting its discipline, without which it can be of no service. Do not, therefore, listen to the partial representations made by children who have been reproved for doing wrong, and particularly abstain from making use of warm or hasty expressions, in their presence, against the master, mistress, or visitors; and if you think you have any just ground of complaint, make it in private to the visitors, who will candidly listen to it. Above all, attend to the disposition of your children, and carefully check, at their very first appearance, any symptoms of passion, sullenness, malice, deceitfulness, or pride. Reason with them affectionately and calmly on the evil of such passions; teach them to act from a reverence to God, and a regard to His authority. Be careful that they say their prayers night and morning : accustom them to spend a few minutes every night before their prayers, in re-collecting their faults, and be frequently reminding them how necessary the favour, and blessing, of God is to their welfare and happiness in this world, and that which is to come. It is by good principles that a good conduct will be promoted, and these principles will be implanted rather by continual watchfulness and affectionate remonstrances, than by angry expressions and severe correction.

By such a system of constant attention at home and at school, it is hoped that your children, under the Divine Blessing, may grow up to be happy in themselves, dutiful to you, and useful to society ; and in due time be prepared for a better world above, when this short and sinful life is ended.

Rules to be strictly enforced by Parents after the Admission of a Child into the School.

1. The parents are requested to send their children punctually at the appointed

time, as strict attention will be paid to their coming exactly to the moment.

2. Every child sent to the school is expected to be clean washed and combed, the hair to be cut short, and the head very clean, without ear-rings or finery of any sort.

3. No child can be permitted to stay in the school, who does not attend regularly.

4. No child is to stay at home without leave from the visitors, except in case of illness, of which notice must be sent to the school, to distinguish whether the absence is occasioned by the fault of the child or not.

5. The parents are expected to submit perfectly to the regulations of the school, and to be willing that their children bear the correction that is considered as necessary to support the discipline of the school.

6. No complaints can be suffered to be made to the master or mistress in the school. If the parents have any to

make, they must make it to the visitors, and it will be candidly attended to.

7. It is earnestly, desired, that parents will take all possible care that their children's conduct be decent and orderly in the streets; and that they will not suffer them to be running about in the evening, after it is dark, or to be playing about on the Sunday.

8. The parents having female children are permitted to send their own, or their children's clothes, to be mended at the school on Mondays, but they must take care that they shall be brought perfectly clean.

9. The children are to attend at school from ten till twelve in the morning, and from two till four in the afternoon on Sundays, until their progress shall render it expedient for them to go to church.

On other days the school hours are from nine in the morning till twelve, and from two till five in the afternoon, excepting Wednesdays and Saturdays, which are half-holidays, when the morning school lasts till one.

Information, Admonition, and Advice, to the Parents and others having the Charge of the Male and Female Children admitted into the Free School, in Orchard Street, St. Margaret's Parish, Westminster.

THIS school has been established upon a new and extensive plan, for the purpose of giving good instruction to a great number of those poor children residing in the city of Westminster and parts adjacent, who, generally speaking, would not have any education at all, were it not for such an establishment.

That no obstacle may stand in the way of attaining the great benefits which this new institution affords, it has been determined by the managers that all *orphans*, and the *children of soldiers*, marines, and seamen in His Majesty's service, shall be educated free of every expense, while all others will be required to pay only the very small sum of one shilling every month*; which is so moderate, that no

---

* Where there are two children of one family, it is only 11*d.* each; if three, the school wages is only 10*d.* a month for each.

parent can have any reasonable excuse, on the score of expense, for withholding from his children the great benefits which they will derive from this institution ; which becomes the more necessary, as experience shows that thousands in these parishes have been ruined, and have become wicked and profligate for want of religious and moral instruction in their early years.

Many of the parents whose children are admitted at present, or may hereafter participate in the benefits resulting from this good institution, have, no doubt, often lamented that in early life they were themselves deprived of the advantages of a moral and religious education ; and therefore, if they reflect at all, they must rejoice in the favourable opportunity which now offers of conferring upon their innocent offspring that good instruction which will preserve them in innocence,—will prove a safeguard against the vices and wickedness which has ruined so many young persons who had not the same advantages, by which parents have experienced great affliction, instead of deriving comfort and assistance from their children after they have become men and women.

All these calamities (and they are almost without number) are to be attributed to the want of religious and moral instruction in early life, and to the bad examples of parents themselves, who having been deprived of good instruction in early life, are unable or unwilling to see the benefits it will confer on their children ; and hence they become disobedient, undutiful, idle, and profligate.

Let every parent reflect, that he or she is accountable to the Almighty Creator of all things for his or her conduct towards their children—that evil example, such as profane swearing, coarse and rude expressions, drunkenness, immoral songs, quarrels and domestic broils, violent passions, indecent discourse, idleness, and lounging in alehouses, are all high offences against the sacred laws of the Supreme Being, and greatly aggravated when they are exhibited to the view and hearing of infants, who are but too apt to imbibe bad impressions, when the evil example comes from their parents, and which never fails to bring ruin and destruction upon the whole family.

It is therefore expected that parents and others who have children under their care, for whom the benefit of this school is intended, will see the necessity of showing a good example to their children, without which it will be in vain to expect much advantage from those excellent lessons of religion and morality which will be given at this school, with a view to make them good men and virtuous women, when they grow up in life; because such bad examples at home will destroy all the good instructions the children receive, and will render it of no use; and by that means defeat all the purposes of this good design for their benefit.

It becomes on this account the bounden duty of all parents and others, having the charge of children, to amend their own lives wherever any thing is amiss, for their own sakes and for the good of their children.— Since no father, mother, or relation, having children under their care, can possibly wish to see them become wicked and abandoned, inasmuch as such wickedness never fails to produce crimes, while crimes are generally followed by disgraceful punishments, and great affliction to parents and relatives.

Let all parents therefore avoid associating or making their innocent infants acquainted with common prostitutes and abandoned and wicked company.—If they wish to be happy and comfortable, let them be sober, virtuous, and industrious : let them spend the Sunday at some place of public worship, instead of debauching their minds in the alehouse, and wasting their earnings, which are allotted for the support of their families. Let the mother of the children do her best to induce the father to love his own home, and his own children, better than the alehouse :—let her always meet him with a smile. Let the house be clean,—the children clean : and let those comforts which are within the reach of every honest industrious man and woman be reserved for the family, which are too often improvidently wasted in the taproom, producing sickness, disease, and misery, merely because they have forgotten religion and virtue—or because they never had it properly impressed on their minds.

Let it never be said that a child shall, with justice, reproach its parents with a neglect of those duties, by which misery instead of comfort and happiness have been the result. Enforce at home the good instruction the children receive at school,—and, above all,

1st. See that all the excellent rules, which are given in a printed paper apart, be attended to, with respect to cleanliness, to punctual attendance at the school, obedience to the master or mistress, and to good behaviour in general.

2d. See that the children, as soon as they get up in the morning, and before they lie down in the evening, repeat the excellent prayers to their Almighty Creator, according to the form which has been given, or will be given, to each of them: and let parents themselves learn, from these duties required from the children, that they too have the same sacred duty to perform.

By following this good advice, the school will become a great blessing both to the parents and the children, because it will not only add to their comfort in this world, but will insure their happiness in that to which every individual is daily, and, in many instances, fast, approaching.

___

At a Meeting of the Committee of the FREE SCHOOL *in Westminster, held at the Committee Room, on Monday, the 16th of June, 1806.*

RESOLVED,

That this Address, containing Information, Admonition, and Advice, to parents and others having the charge of children who are now, or may be hereafter, admitted into this school, be printed, and generally distributed among all concerned.

P. COLQUHOUN, Chairman.

JOHN WILKINSON, Treasurer and Secretary.

___

CONCLUDING OBSERVATIONS.

From the general view thus given of the scheme of education which has been systematized for the children of the poor in Westminster, it will be seen that in addition to the advantages which the pupils are expected to derive, an attempt is made, through the medium of this institution, to contribute to the reform of the parents. It is much to be lamented, that many of them are ignorant, and extremely ill educated, while not a few are, most unfortunately for their offspring, immoral and profligate. The great object, therefore, is to steel the children's minds against the evil examples which are too frequently before them.

These details are also given with a view to induce respectable and philanthropic individuals in the other parishes in the metropolis, and indeed all over Great Britain and Ireland, to adopt a similar cheap mode of education, with a view to embrace as great a portion of the children of the poor as may fall within the compass of private benevolence, that, if possible, the manners and morals of the rising generation may (at least to a certain extent) be improved, and their condition ameliorated by habits of sobriety, industry, and virtue. It is scarce possible to conceive a mode whereby a greater benefit can be conferred on the state, or on the community at large. It embraces almost every object that is useful and important in political economy.

This exposition evinces how much could be done for a very inconsiderable sum of money ; since 1000 children may be nearly as well taught, according to this system, and at no greater expense, than the small number of 30 or 40, who are clothed and fed at foundation charity schools, while both are upon a par in point of religious, moral, and all other useful instruction, when they grow up to an adult state.

Great errors are often committed, and much money wasted in benevolent designs, by taking only a limited, a partial, or an incorrect, view of the object to be attained. The important desideratum is, to compass the greatest possible good at the least possible expense. If ten shillings a year shall convey the same good and useful instruction to the children of the poor, under this new mode of education, as twenty pounds, according to the ancient system of many of the parish charity schools, immense sums are wasted to little purpose, since forty children, in many instances,

might be educated at the expense of one.—
Parents and relations are no doubt glad to
be eased of the burden of feeding and clothing their children, and, in some instances, it
may be right, where there are numerous families ; but it does not always happen that
these are the successful candidates. Interest
and connexion frequently procure admis-
sions where no such pressure exists.

Of the 6000 parish charity children which
are annually assembled at St. Paul's, it may
be fair to presume (as many of them are not
fed, though all are clothed) that in the
teachers' salaries, school rents, stationery,
books, and other expenses, according to the
old mode of education, they cannot cost less
on an average, including their clothing,
than £.10 a year, making an aggregate of
sixty thousand pounds. This sum would
give nearly the same species of education to
120,000 instead of 6000 children, upon the
plan of the Westminster Free School !

Whoever looks accurately, and with the
eye of a political economist, at that portion
of the population of the metropolis and its
environs, which comprises the inferior ranks

of society, will be convinced that there are at all times about 100,000 children, from the age of from 6 to 12 years, requiring that sort of religious and moral education which is suited to their condition in life, and which is indispensably necessary to make them good and useful subjects of the state: and out of this number it may be fairly calculated that at least 50,000 children are reared, and rearing up, every year, in the grossest ignorance and profligacy, and but for institutions of the nature of the one now described, could have no education at all. The situation of the female children under these circumstances is truly lamentable.

That the morals of the inferior classes of society, particularly in the metropolis, are rapidly declining, is evident to every attentive observer; and there is but too much reason to fear that this decline applies to the whole country. What, therefore, must be the situation of the rising generations, under an increased population, if they are reared up under the influence of the grossest ignorance, and of such evil examples, without some counterpoise, some exertion, to check and to prevent the children from becoming still worse than

their parents ?—The prospect is deplorable.—
If the morals of the inferior orders of society
are not of the highest importance to the state
and to the country, it is difficult to discover
in the various ramifications of political economy what is really important.

The extraordinary events which, within
a few years, have taken place on the con-
tinent of Europe,—the important and alarming changes which almost every month, nay,
every week, produces, in their nature and
consequences surpassing every thing which
the history of the world has heretofore re-
corded, at least since civilization and the
arts have been generally disseminated over
Europe, exhibit to the calm and reflecting
mind a state of things so truly awful, that
too much cannot be attempted for the purpose of averting those dreadful calamities
by which neighbouring nations have been
visited. The strength and stamina of every
country exists principally in the mass of the
inferior orders of society ; but for the purpose of giving effect to this strength, upon
which the existence and prosperity of the
state in so great a degree depends, the
morals of this useful class should be guarded

with the utmost jealousy. Without possessing a strong sense of religion and virtue, it is in vain to hope for industry, subordination, or loyalty. To be useful, the great body of the people must also be discreet, sober, and provident. Where it is otherwise, they become the worst of all nuisances in society. Nothing is more certain than that every immoral act has a bad tendency, since immorality is the root of all political evil. An immoral man can never be a good citizen. Yet, true it is, that we should have little reason to complain of the inferior ranks of the community, if more attention were bestowed to form proper regulations for their support and improvement in society. If we suffer them to be ill educated, and then punish them for those very crimes to which their bad education and miserable condition exposed them, the result is, that by such an oversight we make delinquents, and then punish them.

When we consider that the vices of the vulgar are often owing to their deficient education, it is the interest of the legislature, and the higher orders of society, to bestow attention on the means of preventing the effects, by removing, in early life, those causes which produce depravity of manners and generate crimes.

The only means of securing the peace of society is, by enforcing the observance of religious and moral principles. All immoral acts have the same tendency, although some are not so immediate in their effect as others.

The people are to the legislature what a child is to a parent, whose first care ought to be to form the morals of his offspring. But to effect this purpose, legislatures should frame the laws with a view to improve the morals of the people, and thereby not only to teach the parent in vulgar life the duty he is bound to perform towards his children, but to assist them in that duty.

That kingdom is happiest where there is most virtue, says an elegant writer. It follows of course that those laws are the best, which are most calculated to promote morality, since moral virtue is that quality which directs the human conduct intentionally towards the public good.

The most noble, and indeed the primary
ends of society, are to humanize the minds,
soften the manners, and correct the morals
of the individuals, which compose the community. This great desideratum, however,
can only be attained by a proper attention
to the rising generation in vulgar life*.
The object to be accomplished is of the
most incalculable importance. Looking,
however, to the nation at large, it appears
to be too gigantic for the efforts of private
benevolence. The aid of the legislature will
be necessary to give full effect to the design.
The foregoing details have shown it to be
practicable (comparatively speaking) at a
very moderate expense, which would be re-
turned one hundred fold at least to the
community at large in the national wealth

---

* When it is considered that the price of almost all
articles of the first necessity have nearly doubled within
the last sixteen years, and that the wages of the bulk of
the day labourers, in most parts, have not kept pace with
the rapid and unexampled decrease in the value of money,
it is clear to demonstration that that useful class of the
community, called the labouring people, can scarce under
such circumstances, find the means, in many instances,
of supplying even food and clothing for their children;
much less are they able to pay school wages, especially
where the families are large.

acquired by an increased mass of productive labour, and a great diminution of the burdens which are so rapidly increasing, since the records of Parliament show that upwards of one million of individuals, in England alone*,

* According to the Parliamentary returns, made in the year 1803, it appears that the population of Great Britain and Ireland may be fairly estimated, at this time, at - - - - 15,000,000

It has been calculated that the children, or infants, from six to thirteen years of age, requiring education, amount to about one fourth part of the whole population, or - - 3,750,000

From which falls to be deducted one third part, comprising the children of the higher ranks of society, and of parents who are in opulent or easy circumstances, including also the children of tradesmen and others, whose situations in life enable them to allot a certain portion of their income for education - - - - - - - 1,250,000

Deduct also one fifth part for the children educated at public schools, (particularly in Scotland,) and also in workhouses, and at charity schools in Great Britain and Ireland, including, in this calare either wholly or partially supported by the public at large ; a very considerable propor-

Brought over - - - - - 3,750,000	
Brought over - - 1,250,000	
culation, the presumed proportion of children, which virtuous parents in the lower ranks of life struggle to educate at their own expense - 750,000	
	2,000,000

Remains - - - 1,750,000

Which, it is much to be feared, grow up to an adult state, and mix in the national population, *without any education at all,* and also without any *useful impressions of religion or morality.* In this point of view it ceases to be a matter of wonder that so many of the lower orders of the community should be *idle* and *dissolute,* especially when it is considered that many who have even had the advantage of some education, from an inattention to *proper religious and moral instruction,* in ill regulated schools, also become victims to the prevailing vices in vulgar life, and, consequently, become noxious instead of useful members of the body politic.

In the present state of things it is not perhaps too much to say, that every thirty years (the period assigned for a new generation) at least *seven millions* of adults must, in case a remedy is not applied, mingle in the general population of the nation, without any fixed principles of rectitude, and with very little knowledge either of religion or morality. This elucidation, taken in connexion with the great increase of population within the last thirty years, in part at least, accounts for the rapid and alarming declension of the morals of the people, and calls aloud for a peculiar degree of attention to the education of the inferior classes of society in every part of the united kingdom.

tion of whom are reduced to the state of paupers, from profligacy of manners, producing

If farther arguments are wanting to evince the policy, the necessity, and humanity of extending the fostering care of the legislature to the youth of the labouring people of both sexes, and of instilling into their minds in early life, a horror of vice and a proper sense of religious and moral virtue, the aggregate state of the criminals of England and Wales, during the last year, as hereafter detailed, cannot fail to convince the greatest sceptic how much it is the interest as well as the duty of every enlightened member of the body politic to forward by every possible means a general System of Education immediately applicable to the children of the poor.

The criminal offenders committed to the several Gaols of England and Wales, for trial at the superior judicatories, in the year 1805, are detailed from authentic documents as follows:

Males Committed	3267
Females Idem	1338
Total	4605

CRIMES.		CRIMES.	
Sedition	4	Felony and Piracy	7
Murder, in which is included 27 Females, for the Murder of their Infants	53	Arson, or House Burning, &c.	13
		Burglary, and House Breaking	136
Manslaughter	56	Highway Robbery	63
Cutting and Maiming	21	Horse Stealing	65
Shooting at	14	Sheep Stealing	71
Sodomy, Bestiality, and attempts at	15	Stealing Cows and Pigs	38
Rape, and attempt at	38	Larceny, or Stealing from House and Person	3555
Forgery	36	Receiving Stolen Goods	137
Idem of Bank Notes, and uttering, and having	28	Fraud and Conspiracy	94
		Bigamy	23
Coining	15	Returning from Transportation	15
Uttering Bad Money	108		4217
		Brought over	388
Carried over	388	Total	

infirmities, often originating in a bad or immoral education, or in consequence of never

SENTENCES, &c.		EXECUTED	68
Death	350	For Murder	10
Transportation, 7 and 14 years	595	Cutting and Maiming . . .	1
Imprisonment, above 1 and ex-		Shooting at	1
tending to 3 years . . .	128	Rape	5
Imprisonment, 1 year and under	1552	Forgery	6
Whipping and Fines . . .	105	Ditto, and uttering Bank Notes	7
		Coining	3
	2730	Arson	2
Tried and Acquitted	1092	Burglary	15
Discharged, no Bill being found,		Larceny in Houses	2
and by Proclamation . . .	730	Horse Stealing	7
Discharged, to serve in the Navy		Sheep Stealing	5
and Army	53	Highway Robbery	4
	* 4605	Total	68

But, however shocking these details of human turpitude
may appear, they fall far short of the mass of criminality
which afflicts the country, since in this exposition a small
proportion only of the minor offences are included, which are
generally cognizable by the Sessions and inferior courts of
judicature.—In order to ascertain with precision the extent
of the turpitude, the Calendars of the General and Quarter
Sessions, and their Gaol Deliveries, and also the convictions,
commitments, and discharges of Magistrates in the Metropolis, and other populous towns must be taken into the calculation. When the general aggregate is contemplated, nothing can exhibit a more shocking picture of human de-

* Supposing the state of society with respect to criminal offences to remain
stationary—in the course of every new generation comprizing 33 years, 8050
must be condemned to die, about 28,000 (including those sentenced by inferior
magistrates at the Sessions) must be transported, and (when all the judicatories are included) at least 300,000 must suffer Imprisonment, in England and
Wales alone—accompanied in many instances, by Fines, Whipping, and the
Pillory.

having had the advantage of religious or moral instruction in their early years.

It appears from the Parliamentary returns, that in 1803, there were 194,914 of the children of paupers, from 5 to 14 years of age, *permanently relieved* (besides those occasionally assisted, which are equally numerous) by the parishes in England and Wales; and that the whole number educated in schools of industry were only 21,600, most of whom must be very imperfectly taught, when it is consi-

pravity. But even this is not all, since it is well known that of the number of at least minor criminal offences which are committed, perhaps not one in a hundred, or perhaps a much larger proportion (from the lenity of the sufferers, and a dread of becoming prosecutors) ever come under the cognizance of magistrates although actually detected, while those where the offenders are never discovered at all, are infinitely more numerous.—As an instance of this, there are at least 3500 Receiving Houses, or Old Iron Shops, besides a multitude of other receptacles for the same purposes in the Metropolis alone, and yet only 137 have been tried in the superior judicatories in all England and Wales, for receiving Stolen Goods: although perhaps ten thousand small articles unlawfully obtained are purchased in the course of a day. In fact, were it practicable to estimate with perfect accuracy the whole mass of turpitude and acts of criminality committed in the course of a single year, the number of offences as well as the extent of the mischief would excite the utmost astonishment, while it exhibited a melancholy and alarming proof of dered how incompetent to the task the chief part are, who take upon them the duty of teaching the youth of the poor. When it is further considered also that out of a population of 8,872,980 men, women and children, permanently resident in England and Wales, no less than 1,040,716 have been relieved in, and out of workhouses, at an actual annual expense, *applicable to the poor alone*, of £4,267,965—! the importance of giving a right bias to the minds of the rising genera-

the growing depravity of a considerable proportion chiefly of the inferior orders of society, who in many instances are entitled to commiseration and pity, because they have been left without instruction to follow the impulses of unruly and ill directed passions, stimulated by bad examples, and unrestrained by the least sense of religion or moral virtue.

Hence it follows that so many useful subjects are lost to the state by premature death on the scaffold, by transportation, at an enormous expense to the country, and by being rendered idle, useless, hardened and depraved, from the evil habits they contract in gaols.—Hence it is that so many females become prostitutes and thieves, and that 537,139 adults under 60 years of age, and free from bodily infirmity, were in 1803 chiefly supported in, and out of workhouses, at the expense of the Public, whose industry might have been rendered extremely productive to the nation, had not their vices and dissolute manners, by generating idleness and profligacy, thus rendered them nuisances instead of blessings to their country.

tion is an object of the very first importance, since it is but too evident that the great increase of criminal offences, as well as habits of idleness, and the corruption of morals among the inferior classes of society, and the consequent heavy and increasing burden of supporting and assisting such an unexampled proportion of the population, besides the loss of their labour to the community, can be attributed only to a general inattention to the religious education and moral habits of the children of the lower classes of the people.

APPENDIX.

No. 1.

REGULATIONS

For the general Government of the Free School, for the Education of the Children of the Poor, in Orchard Street, Westminster.

1.

THAT the President, Vice-Presidents, and all the Subscribers be invited to assemble on a day and hour to be fixed in the month of May in each year, for the purpose of receiving a Report of the state of the schools, the application of the funds, and all other matters connected with the establishment, and of making such appointments, and giving such orders and directions to the Committee of Managers, as to the general meeting shall seem fit and proper for the benefit of the institution.

2.

That the Committee of Managers shall have the general direction of the establishment, subject to such rules as shall be settled from time to time by the general meetings of the Subscribers. The Committee shall consist of not more than twen·y members, who are authorized to fill up vacancies. The President and Vice-President shall, *ex officio*, be members of the Committee, who shall fix the salaries of the schoolmaster and schoolmistress, and regulate all expenses.

3.

The Treasurer shall receive all monies subscribed and paid for the use of the institution; and shall pay all bills and demands for articles purchased, or repairs made, by order of the Committee. He shall also pay the salaries of the master and mistress, and all other expenses: but no accounts shall be discharged until previously audited, as herein after mentioned.

4.

Three Auditors shall be appointed by the Committee of Managers (two a quorum) who are hereby authorized to audit all accounts and bills, and to signify their approbation by their respective signatures, previous to their being paid by the Treasurer.

5.

The Secretary shall keep an accurate register of all the minutes and resolutions of the General Meetings, and also of the Committee of Managers and Visitors, and shall record all the proceedings relative to the affairs of the two seminaries from year to year, and shall read over the same at the Annual General Meeting.

6.

That five members of the Committee (three a quorum) shall execute the office of Visitors of the school, to direct necessary repairs to be made when previously ordered by the Committee. It will be the duty of the Visitors so appointed to meet at the committee room in the school house, at least once in every month, for the purpose of authorizing the admission of children into the school, above the age of six years, and not more than twelve, excepting in cases where applications are made in behalf of boys and girls above twelve years, and under sixteen, who have already had some education, and will consent to be trained as monitors, or subordinate teachers; but no child' shall be admitted unless accompanied by their parents, and not until previously examined, particularly to ascertain that there is no infectious disease, and also until the parents shall pledge themselves in behalf of their children, that the different laws and regulations of the school shall be strictly observed as far as depends on them to enforce the same. Every member of the committee may attend as Visitors if they shall think fit, and notice shall be given to the parents, or others who have applied to have their children admitted, to attend with them on the day and at the hour appointed by the Visitors.

7.

All children sent by Subscribers, in consequence of written recommendation, stating that they have examined into the circumstances of the parents and children, shall be admitted by the Visiting Committee, without any question, provided their ages exceed six, and are not more than twelve years, and that they are free from infectious diseases—and in all cases where the recommendations of Subscribers are found sufficient to complete the complement of the school, the power of admission on the part of the Visitors shall cease until there are actual vacancies—and no recommendations equal to the number soliciting to be admitted at the time.

8.

The number of boys to be admitted shall in no case exceed 230, and the number of girls 170, making in the whole 400 children. The children of soldiers, marines, sailors in the King's service, and orphans who have no fathers, and in poverty, shall be admitted gratis. The parents of all other children shall pay in advance on their admission—

If one Child only	1s. 0d.	per calendar Month.
If two Children in a family	1s. 10d.	ditto
If three Children	2s. 6d.	ditto
If four Children	3s. 0d.	ditto

9.

The rules laid down for the master and mistress, with respect to the general economy and discipline of the two schools, shall be attended to with the greatest accuracy; since any relaxation whereby a link of the chain may be broken will produce confusion in the whole system, and occasion infinite trouble and anxiety; whereas, by supporting the machine in all its parts the task of superintendance will become easy, and even delightful, to the teachers.

10.

The school shall be examined by the President, Vice-President, and Committee of Managers, with such Subscribers as choose to attend, once in every quarter, namely, on the 5th January, 5th April, 5th July, and 5th October, in each year, when *prizes* and *honorary rewards*, or *medals* and *pecuniary gratuities* shall be distributed to the *pupils*, *tutors*, and *monitors*, according to the number of certificates of merit which they may then produce, and to the specimens they may exhibit of their progress in the different branches of education taught in the schools.—Progress in religious and moral instruction, and uniform good behaviour, to prove always a great recommendation in the distribution of the prizes, with respect to extent and value.

11.

It will be competent for the President, Vice-Presidents, and the Committee of Managers, in their quarterly examinations of the school, to make such further improvements and regulations with respect to the general economy of the school as those examinations may periodically suggest, that the system, thus assisted by practical observation and experience, may by degrees be rendered as perfect as possible.

12.

It will be considered as a duty incumbent on all who promote this most useful design, either as Managers or Subscribers to use their utmost endeavours to give it notoriety, with a view to increase the funds of the institution, and thereby after a time to render it practicable by means of moderate apprentice fees, to procure good masters and mistresses to receive the children as apprentices and servants when they arrive at a proper age, and thereby to prevent the benefits which they have received by strong impressions of religious and moral virtue from being lost to themselves and the community, by idle and vicious habits contracted before they can be placed out in the world.

APPENDIX.

No. 2.

The following is a List of the President, Vice-Presidents, and Managers of the Institution, for the Education of the Children of the Poor, in Orchard Street, Westminster; who were appointed by a General Meeting of the Subscribers, held on the 23d of March, 1804, and subsequent thereto.

The EARL OF GROSVENOR—*President.*

Vice-Presidents.

Right Hon. Lord Chief Baron Macdonald
Rev. Doctor Vincent, Dean of Westminster
Right Hon. George Rose, M. P.
Right Hon. Nicholas Vansittart, M. P.
William Wilberforce, Esq. M. P.
William Smith, Esq. M. P.

Henry Cowper, Esq. (House of Lords)
Rev. Doctor Fynes, Prebend of Westminster
James Stephen, Esq. Barrister at Law
Major General Thornton
Patrick Colquhoun, Esq.
Matthew Martin, Esq.

*Members of the Committee of Management, and
Visitors of the School.*

The President and Vice-Presidents, *ex officio*
Henry James Pye, Esq.
James Hebden, Esq.
Joseph Wilson, Esq.
B. B. Acworth, Esq.
Mr. Matthew Jenkinson
Mr. John Maberly
Mr. Edward Powell
Mr. Richard Sutton
Mr. Benjamin Lucas
Mr. John Bassnet
Mr. William Lucas
Mr. Pitt Cobitt
Mr. Caleb Lucas
Mr. John Hill
Mr. Henry Holland
Mr. John Wilkinson
Mr. William Mucklow.

Mr. JOHN WILKINSON, Secretary, Dartmouth Street, Westminster, authorized to receive Subscriptions; also, Messrs. Drum-
monds, Messrs. Biddulph, Ridge, and Co. Messrs. Ransom,
Morland, and Co. and Messrs. Herries, and Co. Bankers.

Many of the benevolent inhabitants of the City
of Westminster, and parts adjacent, have already
honoured this institution with their support, as
well as some of the Right Rev. Bishops, and
other most resspectable individuals who reside at
a distance. The sums subscribed annually are
optional, and have extended from One Guinea to
Five, while some few donations have been made
to aid the institution at its commencement, from
£.10 to £.25.

The object of the Managers is, to extend the
schools, so as (if possible) to compass in a few
years the education of from 1500 to 2000 children; from a firm persuasion that infants equal
to this large number, in this quarter of the metropolis, must otherwise grow up to maturity,
without either religious or moral instruction.

APPENDIX.

No. 3.

Form of Prayer for Sunday. To be used in the Free School, Orchard Street, Westminster.

[Presented to the Author, by a benevolent Subscriber, and approved by the Managers.]

MORNING PRAYERS.

The Teacher shall begin with these sentences:

JESUS called them unto him, and said, Suffer little children to come unto me, and forbid them not; for of such is the kingdom of God.

Verily I say unto you, whosoever shall not receive the kingdom of God as a little child, shall in no wise enter therein. Luke, ch. xviii. ver. 16, 17.

PSALM.

1. LORD, who shall dwell in thy tabernacle: or who shall rest upon thy holy hill.

2. Even he that leadeth an uncorrupt life: and doeth the thing that is right, and speaketh the truth from his heart.

3. He that hath used no deceit in his tongue, nor done evil to his neighbour: and hath not slandered his neighbour.

4. He that setteth not by himself, but is lowly in his own eyes: and maketh much of them that fear the Lord.

5. He that sweareth unto his neighbour and disappointeth him not: though it were unto his own hindrance.

6. He that hath not given his money upon usury; nor taketh reward against the innocent.

7. Whoso doeth these things: shall never fall.

They shall then kneel, and say together audibly:

Teacher. Lord have mercy upon us.

Children. Christ have mercy upon us.

CHILDREN'S MORNING PRAYER.

O ALMIGHTY Lord God! we thy helpless children bow with the morning light to worship Thee the Father of all the families upon earth, whose mercy hath preserved us from the perils of night and darkness, and raised us to the light and life of another day, another Sabbath; Hallow, we pray thee, this Sabbath in our souls, and sanctify us to keep thy holy day.—Pour upon us thy own good Spirit, without which we can do nothing;—and grant us such a measure of thy grace as shall enable us to learn thy will, and glorify thy name.—Forgive us all our sins, through Jesus Christ, and make us truly sorry for them.—Purify our hearts from pride, stubbornness, and malice; our lips from frowardness, lies, and taking thy holy name in vain.

Behold, O our Father! we come as sinners to our Saviour; blind, to him that hath light; helpless, to him that is mighty; poor, to him that is rich; We pray that as "little children" we may indeed enter thy kingdom, and may that kingdom so come into our hearts, that we may do thy will on earth, and hallow thy name in heaven.

Bless, O Lord, our parents, teachers, and each other,—grant us this day the especial grace of attention, obedience, and instruction; and evermore feed us with the bread of life, that from thy Sabbaths upon earth, we may at last enter into that of everlasting rest in heaven, through the merits of Jesus Christ our Lord. *Amen.*

TEACHER'S PRAYER.

O Lord Jesus Christ, who during thy ministry on earth was pleased to manifest thy peculiar love for little children, regard, we beseech thee, with the same tender compassion those who are now before thee.—Bless this thy "little flock." Sanctify them by thy good Spirit, and inspire them with a constant fear and reverence of thee their Creator, their Redeemer, and their Judge. Feed and nourish them in soul and body unto eternal life; accept their prayers, and hear us when, with one heart and voice, we say as thou hast taught us,

Our Father, which art in heaven, Hallowed be thy Name; thy kingdom come: thy will be done in earth, as it is in heaven. Give us this day our daily bread; and forgive us our trespasses, as we forgive them that trespass against us; and lead us not into temptation, But deliver us from evil. For thine is the kingdom, and the power and the glory, for ever and ever. *Amen.*

THE grace of our Lord Jesus Christ, and the love of God, and the fellowship of the Holy Ghost, be with us all evermore. *Amen.*

EVENING PRAYERS.

Teacher. O Lord our Governor! how excellent is thy name in all the world; thou that settest thy glory above the Heavens:

Children. Out of the mouths of babes and sucklings hast thou ordained strength.—O Lord our Governor; how excellent is thy name in all the world! Ps. viii. ver. 1. 2.

CHILDREN'S EVENING PRAYER.

O ETERNAL God! Searcher of all hearts and Giver of all good, we lift up our infant hands again to thee in thanksgiving for thy mercies [*Here pause to recollect the goodness of God this day.*] We bless thee for our health and strength, the privileges of thy holy worship, and opportunity of learning thy word and law. Pardon, O Heavenly Father, all our sins, and abuse of thy divine benefits. Pardon our indolent spirits, cold hearts, and obstinate wills. Correct every angry thought, malicious purpose, or deceitful intention. That, in humble and teachable minds, as "babes in Christ," we may grow in his grace, and in favour with thee.

Bless all our parents, friends, and benefactors. Forgive all our enemies, and hear the prayers of all who are in trouble or affliction. Take us this night into thy providential care, and fit us for thy kingdom, we beseech thee, through the merits of Jesus Christ our Lord. *Amen.*

TEACHER'S PRAYER.

O ALMIGHTY God, the gracious Preserver of all who trust in thee, bless, we beseech thee, these thy little ones: protect and defend them this night with thy watchful care, and fill them with thy heavenly benediction. Forgive their infirmities, correct their wrong dispositions, and under all the temptations of the world, the flesh, and the devil, be thou, O God, their support and strength. And, O Lord, may both we who teach, and they who learn, ever remember that time when we shall lie down in the dust, and be prepared, whenever it shall be thy good pleasure to call us hence, for that great account, which all of us must render: That, whilst it is yet day, we may so incite each other to love and to good works on earth, that hereafter we may be numbered with thy good and faithful servants in heaven, through Jesus Christ, our Saviour and Redeemer. *Amen.*

Our Father, which art in heaven, Hallowed be thy Name; thy kingdom come; thy will be done in earth, as it is in heaven; Give us this day our daily bread: and forgive us our trespasses, as we forgive them that trespass against us; and lead us not into temptation, But deliver us from evil. For thine is the kingdom, and the power and the glory, for ever and ever. *Amen.*

THE grace of our Lord Jesus Christ, and the love of God, and the fellowship of the Holy Ghost, be with us all evermore. *Amen.*

THE END.

Savage and Easingwood, Printers,
Bedford Bury.